Anonymous

Little Animals described for little People

Anonymous

Little Animals described for little People

ISBN/EAN: 9783337176648

Printed in Europe, USA, Canada, Australia, Japan

Cover: Foto ©ninafisch / pixelio.de

More available books at **www.hansebooks.com**

ICELAND MICE.

THE DOVE SERIES.

LITTLE ANIMALS

DESCRIBED

FOR LITTLE PEOPLE.

BY
THE AUTHOR OF "TRUE STORIES FOR LITTLE PEOPLE."

WITH FOUR ENGRAVINGS
BY HARRISON WEIR.

NEW YORK:
SHELDON AND COMPANY.
BOSTON: GOULD AND LINCOLN.
1870.

THE DOVE SERIES,

IN LARGE TYPE, WILL EMBRACE

THE DOVE, AND OTHER STORIES,

GREAT THINGS DONE BY LITTLE PEOPLE,

LITTLE LILLA; OR, THE WAY TO BE HAPPY,

LITTLE ANIMALS DESCRIBED FOR LITTLE PEOPLE,

LITTLE FACTS FOR LITTLE PEOPLE,

TRUE STORIES FOR LITTLE PEOPLE.

CONTENTS.

LITTLE MICE

RATS

BATS

FROGS

THE HEDGEHOG AND ITS COUSIN

SHREW-MICE

SQUIRRELS

DEAR OLD PUSS

INTRODUCTION.

Did you ever think how all things in this beautiful world of ours speak to us of God, of his greatness, of his power, of his wisdom, of his knowledge, and of his love? When you see the high hills, the tall trees, and the rolling, roaring sea, do you not feel very solemn, and think how great He must be who made all these things? Do you not wonder at his power, and wish you could understand more about it?

I am sure you must have often done so; and when you see that the ground is all dry and hard, and the plants all withering in the hot sun, and that then just when it is so much wanted the rain begins to fall, and everything once more looks fresh and green; you see in this His wisdom and love in providing food for all His creatures. I think you must have often noticed these things; or, if you have not, I am sure you must be one of those little people who, though they certainly have got eyes, yet do not seem to know how to use them. There are many such little folks in the world, and it is not impossible that some of them may read this book. If they do I hope they will find out that one very good way of using their eyes is in looking round on the little animals God has made, and trying to find out some of the wonderful and curious things about them. Seeing the beautiful and perfect way each little creature is made will teach you something about God, about his wisdom and love; it will teach you that he whose power is so great that he can build up mountains, can make the thunders roar and the lightnings flash, and, when it pleases him, can still them with a word; that he who is so great, so mighty, has taken as much pains to make the little squirrel fit for the life it is to lead, or to prepare the tiny mouse for its work, as if they were the most important creatures in the world.

Yes, everything that God does, he does beautifully; and it is that you may see and admire his works that I want you to open your eyes very wide and look about you. And then, besides learning from little animals the love and wisdom of their Creator, we may learn many other lessons from them as well. The Bible tells us to "go to the ant and consider her ways"; to see how industrious she is, and how, though she is a feeble little creature, she lays up food in the summer-time to be ready for the winter, when she knows she shall not be able to find any.

That is one reason why we should watch the ways and habits of God's tiny creatures; but there is another still.

I sometimes see little children who seem to think that the life of a little insect, of a butterfly, or a moth, for instance, is of no consequence; that it does not signify at all whether we hurt or kill them, or what we do to them. Perhaps they think such little creatures cannot feel; if so, they are very much mistaken. These tiny, delicate things are very tender, and very easily frightened; and if you knock them down or catch them suddenly in your hand you have no idea how much pain you may give them. Now, it is God's command that we should be tender-hearted and kind one to another; and I am sure that little children that are really kind and tender-hearted to each other will not be cruel and hard-hearted to God's little creatures.

LITTLE ANIMALS.

LITTLE MICE.

THERE is a little verse in the Bible that I am very fond of, and I should like you to look for it and read it. It is in the twelfth chapter of St. Luke, and the sixth verse. I daresay you have read it before, but perhaps you have never thought much about it; so now I will tell you why I like it so much, and then I think you will like it too.

It tells us that though *we* think the little sparrows that fly about us every day such worthless things, that though *we* take so little notice of them, yet God never forgets even one of them. He knows all about every little sparrow in the world; he knows where they live and everything they do, how long they have been in the world, and when they will die; and he not only *knows* all about them, but he *thinks* about them too. He gives them the food they want, and has taught them how to build their little nests, and how to take care of their little ones.

Now I think it is so nice to know that the great God who made the world, and all that is in it — the great sea, the high mountains, and the beautiful rivers and valleys — that he is so kind and so loving, that he thinks about the tiniest creatures he has made, and cares for them as much as he does for the immense elephants, whales, or any of those great creatures that astonish you so much.

And the more we know of the little animals that we see around us, the more we shall wonder at the beautiful way in which they are made, and the more we shall see how good and kind that God must be who has created them each for some particular purpose and end.

There is one little tiny animal that you must all have seen, for he lives in our own country, and runs about in the houses, in the meadows, in the cornfields, and in the woods. You know what I mean, I daresay: it is the little mouse.

We will talk about it first, because you know more about it than you do about some of the other little animals. But, perhaps, you have not all seen the smallest and prettiest kind of mouse there is. It is the one that lives in the cornfields, and builds its little house among the corn. It is a dear little fellow, all brown except its breast, which is white; but if you want to see it you will have to be very sharp and keep your eyes very wide open, for it is a timid little thing, and would be sure to run away and hide itself if it saw you looking at it.

The harvest-mouse, as it is called, lives on corn chiefly; but it is very fond of insects for a change, especially flies, which it eats very greedily.

This little creature has sometimes a very large family of little ones; sometimes it has as many as eight little baby mice to take care of; but I am sorry to say she is not always very kind to them.

A gentleman who was very fond of watching little animals, had once a little mouse given to him, and in order that he might keep it safely, he had a little cage made for it. In a few days his mouse had eight little children — nice little things she thought them, I daresay, though perhaps *you* would not, for they had no soft hair like their mother, nor bright eyes like hers, but were quite blind when they were first born. At first the old mouse seemed very fond of the little tiny creatures, but she soon got tired of them, and then what do you think the naughty mother did? She really began to kill her little children: was it not cruel? So the gentleman took them away from her, for if she did not love her little ones, she did not deserve to have them at all.

Perhaps you think that when she found they were taken away she would be very sorry she had been so cruel, and would want to have them back again. Oh no; she soon forgot all about them, and was very happy, climbing about her cage, and hanging by her tail from one of the wires.

She had a piece of flannel for her bed, and some grass, which she arranged very cleverly between the folds of her flannel so as to make it soft and quite comfortable, like a feather bed; and then, when she had put her house to rights, she seemed quite happy and contented.

I will not tell you any more stories about their bad habits and their naughty tricks, such as eating each other when they are hungry and cannot find any food; I think it is much nicer to find out something about their busy and industrious ways of gathering together food for the winter.

The little mice you see in the house are not obliged to lay up any stores for the winter, for they live on crumbs and the good things they find in the store-room when everybody has gone to bed, and they can venture out to look for it; but the other mice, which live in the fields, know that when the snow is on the ground and the cold weather has come, they will not find any corn or berries for food, and that unless they wish to die of hunger in the winter, they must get some while they can find it, and keep it till they want it. You see they are prudent little animals; but did you ever think how it is that the little mouse knows that it must do this? It is God that puts it into the little creature's head; it is the great God who says in the Bible that not even a single sparrow can fall to the ground unless he wills it; it is he who gives to the little mouse the food it wants, and teaches it to keep it for the winter.

If you live in the country, and are near any cornfields, you should see if you cannot discover any of the nests of the little harvest-mouse, and then you can watch it gathering together the grains of corn, and carrying them off home and heaping them up in its little store-room; I am sure if you did so you would be very much astonished to see what a deal of work it gets through, just because it never says, "I can't," that silly word that little children are so fond of using, and that so often means, "I don't intend to try."

Perhaps you will say mousie never has such difficult things

to do as you have. Wait a minute: I am not sure of that.

There are some little mice living in Iceland that are obliged, like the harvest-mouse, to store up food for the winter time; and the food which they collect is not very easily found. It is a kind of a berry which does not grow everywhere; and sometimes to get enough they have to swim across wide rivers and take very long journeys. It is quite easy for them to swim across these rivers when they have nothing to carry; but when they are going to return home, and have all their berries to bring with them, what are they to do then? I am sure if the mice asked me what they had better do, I do not think I could tell them. But they do not need to ask any one; they soon make up their minds what to do.

A number of them, perhaps seven or eight, choose a flat piece of dry earth, on which they pile all their berries, making a high heap of them. Then they bring their dish down to the river, pushing it with all their might right into the water, and when it is afloat they all get on, sitting in a circle round the heap of berries, with their tails hanging into the water, and these they move so as to guide their funny boat across the river.

Would you ever have thought of such a capital plan? No, I am sure you would not. But I do not think the mice would ever have been able to do such a clever thing if they had not been very patient and very persevering.

Suppose you take these little creatures for a pattern, and try in everything you do to be as hardworking, industrious, and patient as they are. Shall I tell you how you can do this? I think there are many ways.

Sometimes a little person gets out of bed in the morning, and wants to be dressed very quickly, and then nurse says he must wait, because she is dressing little brother or sister. But somehow or other it is very hard to wait. Then think how often the little mouse has to be patient, and try to be so too; or, if it should happen that a lesson is very hard and long, remember the little Iceland mice, and how hard they work to feed their little ones; and never let it be said that these tiny creatures are more industrious and patient than you are.

RATS.

IN our last chapter I told you something about a very tiny animal, the little mouse, and in this I think you shall hear a little about a creature which is something like it, though much larger, the Rat. It is not a very pretty animal, is it? Few children are very fond of either rats or mice, and sometimes they are very much afraid of them.

But, perhaps, when you have

heard something about them you may change your mind, and begin to take an interest in them. I hope you will, for if you do, I should not be at all surprised if you were to find out something very curious and interesting about them. You would never think that a creature like a rat could have anything like sense, would you? It does not look as if it had much, and yet God has given to this little animal a great deal of cleverness, so that it finds out all sorts of odd ways to get at anything it wants, and seems quite as quick and wise, perhaps quicker and wiser than some little people I know.

Shall I tell you of a funny trick some clever rats played an old lady once upon a time? This old lady had put away in her store-room some bottles of sweet oil, which were packed up in a large box, each one being neatly covered up and fastened. For some time no one wanted these bottles, and no one thought about them; but one day a servant was sent to fetch one, and then she found — well, what do you think she found? Why, she found that the bottles were all uncovered and a great deal of the oil was gone. And who do you think had taken it? Some naughty rats had found out that oil was very nice, and thinking, I suppose, that if they could get at it they might have it, they had helped themselves without asking anybody's leave. And now how do you think they got at it? They could not lift the bottles up and drink it as you would do, and they could not put their noses into them, because the necks were too narrow. I expect you would have said that it was of no use trying to get the oil then; but perhaps these rats knew the song, "Try, try, try again," and were determined not to give up so easily.

One by one they climbed up, and letting their long tails fall into the oil, they drew them out and let the others suck them, so each got a turn and a share of the feast. Were they not clever rats? Should you ever have thought of such a funny plan?

Now, perhaps you do not know that rats do not always stay in one place: sometimes they move, and find a new home for themselves in a new place; and sometimes a great many of them make up their minds to go at once — I suppose because they are sociable, and like being together.

It happened one evening that a gentleman was out walking in the meadows, when he met a company of rats all going in one direction. Now, as he knew a great deal about all kinds of little animals, and rats among the number, he soon guessed what they were doing, leaving their old home, and going to seek another somewhere else, and so he watched them.

In the middle of the crowd of rats he saw one poor old fellow that seemed quite blind and walked very slowly; but that was no reason why he should be left behind; and so when he looked a little closer, he found that one of its friends was leading the poor old rat along by a piece of wood which they held between them in their mouths, and his guide took as much care of him as you would of your papa if he were blind.

I think this shows us that even these little creatures, though they are sometimes fierce and cruel, can love each other very much; and that they try to show their love in much the same way as we do, by helping each other in their difficulties and troubles, for even rats have their troubles, and very great they seem sometimes, I have no doubt.

An omnibus driver once found

a little rat in very great trouble, and squeaking most piteously. What do you think was the matter? Why, just this: his mamma had put him to bed in the hayloft of a stable, and having tucked him up snugly, she had gone out to find some supper, and was a very long time gone, at least so her baby thought. Perhaps he was hungry, and thought it very hard to go to bed without any supper; at all events he began to cry, and was making a very dismal noise when the omnibus driver found him. The man thought he would take the baby rat home to show his children, and so the little fellow was put into his great-coat pocket, and went home with him. He soon grew very fond of the coachman's children, and became their greatest pet; they called him "Ikey," after their eldest brother Isaac; and I am afraid they spoiled him sadly, for he was allowed to go wherever he liked, and do just what he pleased.

Now, there were two things that Master Ikey disliked very much indeed — cold and dirt.

His favorite seat was on the kitchen hearth, but he would only go there when it was very clean; and when in the evening the room got cold, and the wind blew outside, he would lie down at full length before the fire to keep himself warm, and in the night he was sometimes very impertinent indeed, for he would creep into his master's bed, and lie there just as comfortably as if it were his own.

His master taught him many funny tricks; one was to come when he called him, and to jump into his coat pocket, which he held open to receive him. He sometimes stayed there the whole day, going with his master on the omnibus about London; and at other times he sat in the boot of the omnibus, to take care of the driver's dinner. He was a good little rat, and never eat it, unless it happened that there was some plum-pudding in the basket, and then it was quite impossible to resist the temptation; and so, when his master came to look for his dinner, he generally found all the plums gone, and Master

Rat looking very guilty and frightened by the side of what he had left. And no wonder he was frightened, for his master had made a little whip on purpose for him, and when he did not behave properly, it was brought out; and then the little fellow began to squeak most piteously, and would run and hide himself in the darkest corner he could find.

This little rat lived all his life in the coachman's family, and seemed very happy there, and very contented. But though he knew all the children very well, and was never afraid of any of *them,* he always became very shy if any strangers came in, and would never come out of his hiding-place till they were gone, however hungry he might be.

When he began to grow old his teeth became very bad; and the children often laughed to see how distressed he was when any of his food was too hard for him to bite. They used to give him pieces of a very hard cake, made of treacle, which he had always been particularly fond of, just for the fun of seeing him gnawing away with the few teeth he had left, now giving up the task in despair, and then again going at it with fresh courage, not being able to make up his mind to let the sweet bit alone; like some little people who would rather put up with a little toothache than give up those dear but mischievous sugar-plums.

I can tell you another story of a pet rat, if you like: a very cunning rat this one was. A poor man, whose business it was to make whips, had noticed for a long time that some of his pieces of leather disappeared in a very strange way; and especially some long strips which he had cut thin, and covered with oil to make them soft.

Now, he did not like to lose his leather at all; and he watched the box where he kept it very closely, to see if he could find out what became of it. Well, one day he was in his workshop, very busy as usual, when he heard a funny noise in one corner, and when he looked up, he saw a little hole in the wall, and peeping out there was the head of a large brown rat. It looked round very carefully, but when it saw the whip-maker it was afraid to venture out, and ran back into its hole again. The man thought that now he knew who it was that stole his strips of leather; and he determined to watch and try and catch the mischievous creature. So he made a kind of trap, and waited patiently, till after a little while out came Master Rat again, and ran straight to the box where the pieces of leather were kept: in he jumped, and was soon going off with the strip he had chosen, when down came the door of the trap, and shut him in tight.

Then the whip-maker got a thick stick and lifted up the door, intending to kill the little thief as he was trying to make his escape. But Mr. Rat was very cunning, and I suppose that while he was in the trap he thought to himself: " Now I must be very humble, and try and coax that old man not to kill me; I must try and persuade him to let me live, and promise not to touch his leather any more;" and so, when the door was opened, and the man was holding his stick ready to strike his prisoner dead, the little fellow ran out quite boldly, and went straight up the whip-maker's arm, and looked up in his face so coaxingly, and squeaked in such a piteous way, that the man dropped the stick, and taking the rat in his hand he said to it: "Now you know I was just going to kill you, but you are such a nice little fellow that I don't think I will, only you must promise one thing: I will give you plenty to eat every morning, if you will let my leather alone, and not steal any more of it; but if you do, I will kill you." Now I do not suppose Mr. Rat understood all this; but somehow or other he guessed that he must not take what did not belong to him any more; and so from that time he was always contented with the breakfast his kind master gave him, and never went near the box of leather again.

You see from what I have told you that rats are not very dainty creatures; they eat all sorts of things; and if they cannot find food enough they do something which is very naughty. Those that are very big and strong fight with those that are weak, and when they have killed them they eat them up; yes, the naughty rats eat each other up, if they cannot get anything they like better.

A gentleman had once a beautiful white rat, which he kept in a cage; and one day when he went to look at her he found that she had got four little baby rats, all as white as herself. He was very pleased to think he had got five rats instead of one, for white rats are not very common ; but the next day when he went to pay his usual visit to the mother and her children, he found them all gone, and nothing in the cage but a great ugly brown rat. The horrid creature had got in, and gobbled up the poor white rat, and all her little ones.

I am sure five rats must be a great deal too much for anybody's breakfast; and so we must hope he was very ill afterwards, and was taught by sad experience not to be so greedy another time.

You will say, after hearing this story, that rats are very cruel, wicked creatures, and that you do not like them; but I have something still worse to tell you. If a poor rat is taken very ill, and seems as if he would not live, his friends do not nurse him and comfort him, and try to be very kind to him; oh no! they think it much better to kill him at once, and so they set to work and eat him up: What do you think of that? How would you like to be a poor sick rat? Not at all, I expect; for if you are ill you like to be nursed, and petted, and kissed; you like to feel that other people are sorry, and would make you well if they could; but the rats do not seem to pity their poor friends at all; they only seem to think that as he is ill they shall have very little trouble in killing him, because he is not strong enough to defend himself.

However, we must not be too angry with them for their cruelty to their sick brothers and sisters, for we must remember that there are some places in the world where men and women do just the same thing, and that is much worse, because they ought to know better.

There are many things that are very interesting even in the fierce rats. It is very nice to see their love for their little ones, and their clever ways of getting their food; and sometimes, like little Ikey, they make very good and loving pets.

A BAT AND HER BABY.

BATS.

ALL little children are fond of little birds, and so I suppose you are too. You like to hear their different songs when you wake in the morning, to watch them leaving their nests in search of something for their little ones' breakfast, or teaching them, when they are old enough, to fly, and to take care of themselves. You like to see them, and you often say how pretty they are: the robin with his red waistcoat; the blackbird with his yellow beak; the swallow with his black and white coat; and hosts of others, of all colors and shapes. But did you ever think why God made the little birds? Did he only make them to look pretty and to amuse us with their sweet songs? Oh, no; it is quite true that when he gave them such beautiful voices he did it partly that they might cheer us, and make us feel glad and happy, as I am sure they often do; but that is not their only work. Do you know what is the food of these little birds? They do not live only on seeds and on the grains of corn they can pick up in the fields, but they like to have some meat too; and so they catch the flies and gnats, and other insects which fly about in the summer-time, and make their dinner off them.

And by eating all these little creatures they do a great deal of good. If they did not do so there would be so many flies, so many gnats, so many wasps, and so many caterpillars that we should not know what to do.

This is the work of the little birds; but I am not going to tell you about any kind of bird to-day, but about a little creature who helps them very much.

You know that when the sun has set, and the moon comes out, and the night covers the earth, the little birds think that it is time to go to bed; so they leave off their work and go to their little nests, and there they put their heads under their wings and are soon fast asleep. But in the meantime all the insects have not gone to bed;

some of them are very busy still; indeed, I think the gnats come out the most in the evening; and then it is that the little bat appears, all brisk and lively, to begin his work just where the swallow had left it off.

Did you ever see a bat? If not, go to the window any warm evening in the summer-time, after it is dark, and you will be almost sure to see one, flying about in very much the same way as the swallow does in the daytime. But I do not promise you that you will see much of its shape, for the little thing flies so fast, now close to the ground, now high up among the trees, now almost touching you, and the next minute quite out of sight, that it is almost impossible to see what it is like while it is flying, and when it is not on the wing it does not look half so pretty.

But perhaps you want to know whether the bat can sing like the birds. Well, it certainly can sing, but its voice is not very pretty. I will tell you what it is like: if you take a slate pencil with a very sharp point, and holding it as upright as you can, draw it quickly down your slate, it will make a noise very like the note of a bat, only nothing like so shrill and sharp.

Do you know that some people are so silly as to be afraid of these pretty little creatures, and will never touch them if they can help it? A poor little bat once flew by mistake into a grocer's shop, and as he could not find his way out again he tried to hide himself behind a pile of sugar-loaves on a high shelf. Now the grocer, foolish man, was afraid to touch him, and so he sent for a gentleman who lived near, and who he knew was very fond of little animals, to come and catch his bat for him. The gentleman was very willing, and taking with him an old cage he went to the shop. There he found Mr. Bat squeezed up as small as possible into a corner, but when he tried to take hold of him the creature flapped his wings and tried to escape; but his enemy was stronger than he was, and soon made him fast prisoner.

This little fellow had got sharp little teeth, and tried hard to bite: but he soon found it was no use, and that he must submit to being captured and put into the wooden cage.

As soon as he was safe inside, he began climbing up the back, and hung on by his claws from the top, having his head downwards; a very uncomfortable position, I should say; but bats always seem to like it best.

This little creature was a dainty bat, and instead of eating insects whole as most of them do, it would pick them to pieces, and only eat the parts it liked best. And the same with the pieces of meat that were given to it; if they were at all hard or dry, nothing would make it touch them.

This poor bat did not live long in its wooden cage. I daresay it was not so happy as it would have been flying about in the open air; or perhaps it had been hurt when it first flew into the grocer's shop: anyhow, it lived only two or three weeks, and was found one morning hanging by its hind claws from the roof of the cage, quite dead.

It is not a very easy thing to keep these tiny animals alive in prison; they are so fond of flying about, and doing just what they like, that when they find themselves shut in tight, and that they cannot get out, they often grow very unhappy and gloomy, and die in a few days. Five large bats were once caught in a country town; four of them were lady bats, and the other was a gentleman. They were put into a large cage, and were fed with everything that bats generally seem to like. But they all looked very melancholy, and would not touch their food, thinking, I daresay, that it would be much nicer if they had caught it themselves. The gentleman bat was very cross indeed, much worse than any of the ladies, squeaking ~~most dismally~~, and biting the others whenever they came near, and breaking his teeth by trying to gnaw through the bars of his cage.

At last, one day, he died, I suppose, of a broken heart; and then the others began to forget how unhappy they were, and grew more cheerful and contented. I daresay they were very glad to be rid of cross Mr. Bat, who had made himself so disagreeable; and for a few days the four ladies lived together very happily.

But, one by one, three of them died, and only one remained; but she grew very tame, and used to spend all day hanging by her hind feet from the top of the cage, coming down when it began to grow dark, and flying about quite merrily.

She also took great pains to clean herself, combing out her

hair with her claws, and seeming particularly anxious to have a very nice straight parting down her back. In a few days she had a little baby bat, and now how do you think the mother would nurse her little child? She had a very funny way of nursing it. *She* did not hold it, but *it* held her. Is not that strange? But you know I told you that the old bat used always to hang from the cage by her claws with her head downwards, and as the little one liked to do so too, she taught it to fix its tiny claws into her body, and to hang on to her in the same way as she hung to the cage. She liked to have it very close to her, for she was very fond of her baby, and took a great deal of care of it.

But after two days the mother died, and the poor little bat was left an orphan. The gentleman to whom the bats belonged was very much afraid it would die too, now that it had no one to take care of it, so he wrapped it up in flannel to keep it warm, and fed it with a sponge dipped in milk. But it was of no use; the little creature could not do without its mother, whose fur had kept it so nice and warm, and after eight days it died too.

So it is very plain that these pretty little creatures do not like to be shut up in cages, and made prisoners, instead of being allowed to spend their lives in flying about in the beautiful open country, so happy and so busy doing the work for which they were made; and though I think you should try all you can to find out all about these curious little creatures, I do not think you would like to shut them up in a cage, because you know how much happier they would be if they were free and wild as they were before they were caught.

Is there any lesson we can learn from the little animals? Let me see: I think there is. The little mice taught us to be industrious and to work hard; and now the bat adds a little piece on to that lesson. It tells us that we are to do our work not only with all our might in the day-time, I mean when people can see us, but to do it just as well when there is nobody to see and nobody to praise us for our industry.

I said nobody to see, but yet there is Somebody. There is One who sees in the dark as well as in the light, to whom the night is as clear as the day: the great God who made the little bats, and who sent them forth to do their work in the night-time, to fill up the gap the swallow leaves when it goes to bed in the evening.

Yes, He sees, and we should never forget that.

FROGS.

WE were talking in the last chapter about a baby bat, and about the great care its mother takes of it, but in this we are going to see if we can find out anything about a creature whose mother takes no care of it at all when it is little, but leaves it to manage for itself altogether. Did you ever notice when you have been near the side of a pond, some masses of little eggs about the size of a pea, which float on the surface of the water, generally lying among the long grass at the edge of the pond? I daresay you have seen them sometimes; but perhaps you never thought of asking what they are, or anything about them.

Well, suppose you were to come back again in a few days to the same place, do you think you would find these dark-looking eggs still there? Ah no; they would be all gone; and in their places you would see numbers and numbers of funny little black creatures with very big heads, and flat thin tails, which make them look something like fishes. These little black creatures are called tadpoles; they grow very fast, because they eat a great deal, and in a little while the long thin tail disappears, little legs grow instead; and the animal is no longer a tadpole, but a little frog, jumping about just as you have often seen frogs do.

Now, if you were to ask the little frog where he would like to live, and if it could answer you, what do you think it would say? Why it would say, "Oh!

let me stay here by this pond, where the ground is so nice and wet; I like to have plenty to drink, I am always so thirsty." And if you did not listen to the little frog, but took it away to a place where there was no water and where the ground was dry, it would soon grow very thin and die, for of all animals the frog is the most thirsty. It does not only drink with its mouth, but it sucks up water through a great many little holes in its skin, just like a sponge does if you put it in a basin of water.

A gentleman once caught a number of frogs, which he kept in a bowl of water; as long as there was plenty of water in the basin, they looked very fat and well; but if he took them out when the weather was very hot they soon grew thin and ill. These frogs grew quite tame, and learned to take their food from their master's hand. They were very fond of flies, and were very clever at catching them; so, when the fruit for the gentleman's dessert was laid out in the storeroom, these frogs were placed round it, to act as little policemen, and keep the flies from spoiling it; and they did their work very well indeed.

So as the frog likes a great deal of water, and is very fond of the insects that he finds in it, I think it is quite right that he should stay in the water, or as near it as he likes; for though of course they are very useful animals, and do a great deal of good by eating the slugs and other insects which are very troublesome if they get into cornfields or gardens, still I cannot say that I should like to have a frog for a pet, or even a toad, which is its first cousin, you know.

So I say I think they had better stay down in the ponds and rivers, and let us go and visit them there, instead of coming to see us at home, where they are never very welcome. Now there are some very funny things about the frog which you should look out for when you go to see it.

One is that after it has worn its coat for some time, and thinks it is either getting very tight or very shabby, it makes up its mind to get rid of it; as this is a very curious ceremony I will tell you about it. When a number of frogs have determined to change their skin, having, of course, got new ones underneath, several of them begin at once. Two of their companions hold the one whose coat is to come off, tight round the middle of his body, while one or two others give little bites and pulls at his skin, till by degrees, first one leg, and then the others, and at last the whole body is set free, and the frog appears with such a clean white skin that I am afraid he must be very vain.

If there are many of these little creatures changing their coats at the same time, and in the same pond, as there are sometimes, they make quite a loud noise with their croaking, so that you would almost fancy that there were some ducks in the pond.

I have told you that frogs are very thirsty creatures, and like to live in damp places; but I must not forget to tell you about one frog who was different from most of his relations in this respect, that he always chose out warm and dry places for his house.

He had made his way into a gentleman's house by a hole in the wall of the kitchen; and though for a long time he was very shy and timid, and never dared to leave his hiding-place when any one was in the room, yet after a time he forgot all about his fears, and came out regularly every day to be fed.

His favorite seat was close to the kitchen fire, where he used to sit for hours in the long winter evenings; and, being a great friend of the old cat, he would often nestle himself under her fur, she all the while making no objection, but seeming quite fond of her strange companion. How it happened that this little fellow had such a dislike to the cold I do not know, for, as I said before, most of his brothers and sisters seem to be all alive in damp, chilly weather, and anything but happy if the sun is very hot.

But before I finish this chapter I must tell you of a dreadful scrape in which poor frog once found himself.

In taking his usual morning walk, this little fellow made a mistake, and taking a rather longer jump than usual, he found himself close to a cage full of monkeys, grinning and chattering, and looking horribly mischievous. Before he had time to get over his fright enough to get out of their way, one of these mischievous little animals was down on the ground, and putting his paw between the bars, he pulled poor froggie into the cage. Oh, what a fright he was in! He expected every moment to be bitten in two, and swallowed down. But no; none of the monkeys knew what to make of the cold, wet creature; and they hardly liked to touch it; so one of them held him up by the end of one leg, while all the rest stood examining him, to see what could make him feel so very strange. All the while the poor old fellow was half dead with fright, and tried to show by his struggles how uncomfortable he was, and how much he wished they would let him go. At last his kicking became so violent that the monkey let him fall, and without losing any more time the frog picked himself up and hopped off as fast as he could, quite determined never to go too near a monkey's cage again, as long as he lived.

Poor frogs sometimes get into trouble and into great difficulties in their battles with other creatures. I have told you that they themselves live on insects, flies, snails, and worms, but I do not think I have told you that they are themselves eaten by larger animals. A gentleman was once walking through a field, when he heard a very loud croaking, as if a poor frog was in great distress somewhere near. The sound seemed to come from a ditch not far off, so he went to see if he could find out what was the matter; and there he saw a large snake having a great battle with a fine fat frog.

Mr. Snake had got the best of the fight, so far, and was trying to swallow poor froggie, having got his fore legs into his mouth, and pulling away with all his might to get the hind ones in too. The poor frog, however, had a great dislike to being treated in this way; to be swallowed alive, the very idea was so horrible; so with all his strengh the struggled to get free, croaking all the while as loud as he could, I daresay in hopes some brother frog might hear and come to help.

No brother or sister, however, was to be seen; but the gentleman who was watching the fight happened to make a little noise, which frightened the snake so much that he dropped the poor frog and made off as fast as possible.

The poor fellow could hardly believe that his horrid enemy was really gone, and that he was safe in the ditch once more. It seemed too good to be true; but yet the snake was nowhere to be seen; so, after waiting a little while to recover himself, for he was still feeling rather queer and uncomfortable, he hopped off again to his hole, thinking, I daresay, what very disagreeable creatures snakes are, and hoping he should never meet one again.

Now I have told you a great many funny things about frogs,

and I have shown you, too, that though they are not very pretty animals, they are useful ones. They do a great deal of good by eating the little slugs and insects which spoil the flowers and vegetables in our gardens; but that is not their only use.

In some countries people eat the frogs, and like them very much; and I daresay if you were to go to France, you might like them very much too; for though we do not eat them in England, and think it is very strange for anybody to do so, the French people like them very much, and say they are quite as good as a chicken when they are nicely cooked; and they give them to sick people who cannot eat anything but very nice food.

THE HEDGEHOG AND ITS COUSIN.

I SAID something at the beginning of this little book about the great care and love with which God watches over his smallest creatures. I showed you how he teaches the little mice to lay up their food for the winter, so that they may not be starved when the cold weather comes, and they cannot find any food; and, in the same way, when we were talking about the bat, I told you how

THE HEDGEHOG AND THE SNAKE.

the timid little thing that cannot venture out in the daylight, finds its food all ready for it, when the sun having set, and all around being dark, it creeps out from its hiding-place in some old barn or church tower, and begins its evening flight.

And so with all the other little animals that I have been telling you about: we see, in many different ways, the tender love of the great God for all the things that he has made; and in the life of the little hedgehog the same thing is very plain.

Have you ever seen one of these little animals? If so, you know that it is not a very pretty creature; it has a coat all over things very like long thorns, which are called spines; and it is with these that the hedgehog defends itself from all its enemies.

For it has a great many enemies. The weasel, the marten, the polecat, and many large birds often fight with it, and try and kill it; but they very seldom succeed; for as soon as they begin their attack, the hedgehog rolls itself into a ball, covering its head with its prickly spines, and then no animal dares to come near it: and no wonder they keep at a distance; for I daresay you have sometimes put your hand for a moment into a thorny rosebush, or gooseberry bush, and know how it feels, and how fast you draw it back again, and how many scratches you find on it when you have got free from the thorns. Now, if it had not this spiny coat, the little hedgehog would be quite unable to fight with all the fierce animals that attack it; for it cannot, like some of the creatures you have read about, run away and get out of their reach. It cannot move fast, and is very clumsy and awkward; and so this is why God has given it such a thick thorny coat to protect it, just as the coats of mail were made to protect the soldiers long ago. But though the hedgehog has so many enemies, it is not at all a fierce creature itself. It generally feeds on worms and insects, and lives in a hole in the ground at the root of a tree. Sometimes people catch hedgehogs and keep them in the kitchen to kill black beetles and other insects; and sometimes they grow very tame, and even catch mice as well as cats do.

It seems funny to think that such queer-looking creatures can ever be tamed; but it is quite true: and sometimes they grow quite fond of their masters, and like to be petted and caressed. I heard of one once which would stretch itself out, and lie on its master's knees before the fire, letting him stroke that part of its face that has no spines, and evidently liking to feel the touch of his hand.

Another grew so tame that it made friends with an old terrier dog, and the two would lie together before the fire, nestling close together that they might keep each other warm. And they did not, like some little people I know, soon forget their love for each other, and begin to quarrel; but they continued to be the best friends in the world as long as they lived.

Now, though I said the hedgehog generally lives on worms and insects, and does not often kill anything larger, it does sometimes eat small snakes; but then it must be a very bold hedgehog that will dare to fight with a snake.

A gentleman once saw a very fierce battle going on between a hedgehog and a snake; and it was very funny to see how cleverly the little fat creature attacked its slippery enemy. Watching its opportunity, it quickly unrolled itself, and gave the snake a sharp bite; but before it could be hurt in return, it had again turned into a round spiky ball, so that the poor snake was quite puzzled what to do. While he was wondering, the hedgehog again uncurled itself, and with another bite, breaking the back of its enemy, gained a complete victory. And now there was nothing for it to do but to begin its dinner, and so it set to work. First it passed the whole body of the poor snake through its teeth, breaking the bones at each bite; this was the hedgehog's way of dressing its dinner. It did not want a saucepan to boil it, or a fire to roast it, nor anything to make it nicer than it was; for to our little friend I daresay a whole snake was a very great treat; anyhow, it eat it all up, and seemed to enjoy it very much.

There is one animal, however, that can kill the hedgehog in spite of its spines and its clever way of defending itself. The fox, as you know very well, is a most cunning creature; and he is the worst enemy of the little hedgehog; for he has found out how to make it unroll itself, and when that is done, it is very easy to kill it. I daresay that even Mr. Fox was very much puzzled at first; but when we look at his sharp face, and little round twinkling eyes, we can easily believe all that people tell us about his being so sly, so mischievous, and so cunning.

Now, the fox is too wise, a great deal, to go near those sharp thorns and get his nose pricked; oh no: he knows better than that. He sees that though the hedgehog has covered its head safely, yet its feet are left bare; and so, running at them, he gives them a little bite with his sharp-pointed teeth, just hard enough to make it uncurl itself; and then he knows he can do what he likes with it, for then it is quite helpless and defenceless.

No wonder, then, that the hedgehog is so much afraid of the sharp, clever fox, when even the thick armor that God has given it for defence cannot protect it from his attacks.

But you have heard quite enough about the hedgehog, and we will now go and see one of its cousins, a funny little creature that lives underground, and very seldom comes up into sight. Perhaps it does not like the light, for it has very tiny eyes, so small indeed that they can hardly be seen; so it makes its house underground, feeding on those long worms which I daresay you have often seen crawling about in the garden.

Now, it seems to us very strange that any creature should like to live in a hole in the earth where the sun does not shine, and where everything is so dark; I am sure no little child would choose such a home—so dismal, gloomy, and cold. Why is it, then, that the little mole picks out such a place in which to build his house? I think there is a very good reason. You know that God has made every one of his creatures for some particular purpose, and has given to each the work that it has to do. He made the horses, cows, and sheep for our use; and what should we do without them? And the smaller creatures too have all their different work to do. And what is the little mole's business, do you think? Have you ever noticed little heaps of earth on the garden flower-beds, beaten down and patted very smooth? Well, this is the mole's house, and from this heap there are many little tunnels running in different directions: it is in these little passages that the mole catches the worms for its food.

Now this funny little house, with its tunnels and passages, is like a drain, and carries away the water which would very likely injure the roots of the plants if it were left there too long.

This is the work that the mole is busy about all its life;

and this is why it always lives underground. So when you see the little mounds of earth in the garden you will know that the little animal that is hidden below them is working hard to do its Maker's will; and I hope the sight will make you say to yourself, "Am I as busy serving God and doing what he tells me to do as that little mole is?"

A mole seems a funny creature to pet, and yet a gentleman kept one once that he might watch it at its work. At first he could not find anything that would do for its house; but at last it was put into a very large tub filled with earth, for you know it would not live if it had not some earth in which to bury itself.

As soon as it found itself in the tub it sank instantly out of sight; and though its master wanted very much to see it at work, it would never come above ground; and the only way in which he could watch it was by digging it out, and letting it run along a hard gravel-walk.

You would think it would be

pleased to get free to have a run in the bright sunshine after having been so long in the dark, underground; but no: directly it was loose it began trying to find a place soft enough for a tunnel, by which it might hide itself again deep down in the earth. Several times, when it had nearly succeeded, it was dragged out again; but at last it slipped off the path on to a soft place, and in an instant was gone quite out of sight. They tried to dig it up again, but it could dig faster than any spade, and so the pet mole was never seen any more. Now, these little animals are not very sociable; though they have such beautifully made little houses underground, they keep them all to themselves, and if another mole were to come in and try to make his house in the same hill as one of his friends, he would either be driven out very quickly, or there would be a very fierce battle to decide who should be master; and the two little animals would go on fighting till one or other of them was killed.

You would not have thought that that black, stupid-looking creature could be so savage, would you? but it really is one of the fiercest of animals, and, except when it is asleep, it spends the whole of its time hunting for insects and small animals for food, venturing into all sorts of dangers without the least fear, if there is a chance of finding some prey.

It will even go into the water, and swim boldly across a stream, if the creature it is chasing is a water animal; for, besides being able to dig so well, the mole is a first-rate swimmer; his feet are more like hands than claws, and do just as well to help him in swimming as in digging.

So God has provided for all these creatures' wants. They live almost altogether underground, in the dark; so he has given to them very weak, small eyes; but if they cannot see well, they have very sharp ears, and can hear the least noise made by a worm creeping near them, or by an insect buzzing near the entrance of their holes.

SHREW-MICE.

PERHAPS you would never have thought that the little creature you see in the picture could be any relation to the clumsy, fat hedgehog you have just been reading about, or to the groping, digging little mole; but it really is very nearly related to both of them.

Look at its pointed nose; is it not something like that of the hedgehog? And if it would open its mouth and show you its teeth, you would see they are very sharp and pointed, just like those of both its cousins.

Now, though this little animal is called a shrew-mouse, you must not think it is at all like the little creatures which we were talking about in the first chapter, — the little mice you have so often seen running about; or, if you have not seen them, for they are very timid, and do not like to be seen, I am sure you must have often heard them.

But the little shrew-mouse is a very different creature; it lives in the fields, and may be often seen hunting for and feeding on the insects and worms which are its food.

Now, it is a very innocent little animal, and never does any harm, and so nobody is afraid of it; but a long time ago everybody thought it was a poisonous animal, and did a great deal of harm.

They really thought that if this pretty little thing touched the body of a cow, or a horse, or any other animal, it would hurt it very much; and if any of these creatures were taken ill they were always quite sure that it was because a little shrew had touched it, or run over it.

That was very silly, was it not? And the way in which they tried to cure the sick animal was still more foolish, and, what is worse, very cruel too.

They used to look for an ash tree, and when they had found one, what do you think they did? They made a little hole in the side of the trunk, and having taken prisoner a poor little shrew, they put him alive into the hole in the tree, and then fastened it up tight, so that he could not get out, but died from want of air.

What could be the use of treating him so cruelly? What good could it do to the cow or the horse that was ill? None at all, of course; but these silly people thought that the leaves of the tree in which the poor shrew died were the best medicine the invalid could have, and were quite sure it would get well directly it had eaten some of them.

Perhaps you may have seen some very old trees in different parts of the country, which are called shrew-ashes. There is one in Richmond Park: it is very much broken, and has not many leaves on it, and I daresay will not live very much longer; but if you should ever see it, you will remember what I have told you about these trees, and the poor little shrews who were so cruelly killed in them.

But this is not the only kind of shrew there is. You remember I told you that this one lived in the fields and fed on worms; but there is another shrew that lives in the water, and eats the insects and little fishes which it finds there. Both these little creatures have very pointed noses and long tails; but the one that lives in the water has a very nice smooth coat, very like the coat of the mole, and when it comes out of the pond where it has been swimming about, it looks as shiny and silky as if it were made of velvet.

This little creature seems to lead a very happy life. It is so lively and merry, it has so many funny ways, and is always so busy and active, that I think it can hardly have time to be unhappy.

If you were to find out a place where these shrews live, down by the edge of a pond, and were to sit down near it to watch them, you would see many things that would amuse you, and you would almost forget that they are only little mice, and have not the sense you have, when you see the games they play, and all their funny tricks.

They are very much afraid

of large animals, and especially of men; and though you are very small, and would make very little noise, still, if you speak or laugh, they will all run away as fast as their little legs will carry them. But if you are very quiet, they will not find out you are anywhere near, and then you will see them swimming about in the water, chasing the insects, and especially a large water beetle which they are always very anxious to catch, for it is their favorite food; and then when they have caught it, they do not eat it in the water, but bring it safely ashore, and having found out a nice dry stone, they sit down to take their dinner comfortably. And now see in what a funny way they eat. They do not lay the insect down on the stone before them, and bite it while it lies on the ground, but they take it up between their two fore-paws, and, holding it very tightly, as if they were still afraid it might escape, they begin their feast.

And then, when dinner is over, and they have had a little

nap, they all go out for a walk, or rather for a run, for the water-shrew is such an active little fellow that he does not often move slowly, but runs as fast as such tiny feet can possibly go. Well, their walk is generally backwards and forwards by the edge of the pond; and when they pass each other in their turns, they both give a sharp cry, as much as to say, "Good-morning," or, "How do you do?" just as you would do if you met a little friend in your walks.

A gentleman was walking

one evening in his orchard, a little before sunset, and watching the flies and insects swimming about in a little pool of clear water, when all at once he saw something that looked like a very large beetle dart through the water, and disappear in the grass on the bank.

He waited a little while to see if it would come out again; and very soon he spied it leaving its hole, and, diving under water, bury itself among the leaves at the bottom of the pool, and then he saw that it was a little shrew-mouse. After staying there a few minutes it came up again, and once more went to its hole in the bank, most likely to eat some insect it had caught among the mud and leaves under water. Several times it went backwards and forwards, but it always seemed very timid, and dived under water at the least noise.

This little creature did not live alone in the pool: it had a mate just like itself, only much more slender and delicate looking, her coat too being of a lighter brown.

The gentleman used often to

look for them when they came out of their hole in the evenings, for they were never seen in the daytime; and to watch their graceful movements in the water, and to listen to their short, sharp cries to each other, was his great delight for some months, and very sorry indeed he was when, about the end of May, they both disappeared, and he never saw them again.

The little water-shrew has one great enemy, and that is the weasel. This long, thin creature lives on small animals, and it often chases the little shrew, and frightens it very much; but if it is near the water, it can always escape by diving below the surface, where the weasel cannot follow it.

What a good thing it is for the little shrew that it knows how to dive! and how kind and wise that great God is who knows all the dangers and wants of all these tiny animals, and takes such care of them!

SQUIRRELS.

WE have been talking about many different little animals, all of them very curious, and some of them very pretty and interesting; but I think there is one that is far prettier than any we have had yet, and that is the little Squirrel.

I should think that most of you must have seen a squirrel at some time or other, either a tame one in a little round cage, or a much happier wild one living in the woods among the tall fir trees. If you have only seen them shut up in a cage, you do not know much about them, for there they look the most quiet creatures in the world, as if they cared for nothing but twirling round and round all day long, making one feel quite giddy to look at them; but if you saw them in the woods where they were born, and where they ought always to be, you would say that they are the happiest, merriest little animals you have ever seen; and so they are.

Some years ago, when I was staying in the country, it happened that close to the side of the house where my bedroom was, there grew some tall fir trees, the long branches of which used almost to touch my window, and in these trees, sheltered from the cold by their dark, thick leaves, some dear little squirrels had made their home.

Wild little animals they were indeed, but oh, so happy!— How any one can shut up those merry little things in a tiny cage, so small that they can hardly turn round in it, I never can imagine. I used to love to watch them as they ran along the long, thin branches which shook beneath their feet; coming so close to the window that they could almost peep in, and say, Good-morning; and then, if I made any noise, scampering off again with their tails over their backs, and their bright eyes twinkling, to hide themselves in some dark part of the tree. But though squirrels are generally very timid, these little friends of ours seemed to have found out somehow or other that we would not hurt them; and so they grew very bold. There were some fine chestnut trees on our lawn before the dining-room window; and the squirrels were not long in finding them out, and in making frequent journeys to them when the nuts were ripe. Now we, too, were fond of chestnuts, and would have liked to keep some for ourselves; but, unfortunately, we could not climb like our little friends, and so our share was very small. For they would run across the gravel-paths, scamper over the lawn, and be high up in the trees before we could get near to frighten them away; and often and often I have seen the little things perched on the very highest boughs, cracking the nuts with their sharp little teeth, or carrying them off with great delight, to be hidden in some safe place till they were wanted in the wintertime.

And where do you think their store-rooms are? Either a hole deep in the ground, or in the trunk of a tree, serves for a cupboard to keep their food in till the cold weather comes; for, like the little mouse, the squirrel is obliged to save up some of its summer food to eat in the winter. The nuts which it can find so easily in the autumn, and the corn in harvest-time, are what the squirrel loves best; and this is why God has given to it such active little feet, and taught it to climb and run so well. And so, when it sees the snow on the ground, and hears the wind making such a noise among the trees, the little squirrel is not afraid that it will die either of cold or hunger, for it has plenty of food to last a long while; and such a warm coat, and such a nice little nest, that it can put up with a good deal of cold, even though it has not a fire as you have.

Now, sometimes this prudent little animal does not hide its nuts and acorns all in the same hole. Sometimes it digs a hole for each nut and each acorn; and then, as it buries so many every year, it is hardly likely that it can remember where it has put them all.

A lady was walking about in a wood, when she noticed a squirrel sitting at the bottom of a tree; it was so busily occupied that she stood still to watch it, and in a few moments it darted like lightning from the ground, and in an instant was at the top of the tree beneath which it had been sitting.

After staying a few minutes, she saw it again on the ground, holding an acorn in its mouth. It instantly began to dig a hole in the ground with its paws, and when it was big enough, the acorn was put in, and neatly covered up with earth.

It then returned to the tree, bringing down another acorn, and this it did many times till it had safely buried a great many. And do you think it would find them all again? Oh no! I daresay many of them would be dug up and eaten in the winter; but still most likely it would lose a few, and then, what would become of them? Why, they would grow up into great tall trees, oak trees, bearing acorns to feed other squirrels, perhaps the great-grandchildren of the very squirrel who hid them, little thinking what would become of them.

A great many of those tall oak trees, which make our woods look so beautiful, have, I daresay, been planted by these tiny animals: and so, without knowing it themselves, they are very useful to us; for besides the cool shadows which the thick leaves of the oak cast for us on a hot sunny day, it is a very valuable tree because of its wood, of which so many useful things are made.

Now, when we see how happy and useful the little squirrel is in the woods, it always seems to me very cruel to make pets of them, and shut them up in cages. They may grow contented, and perhaps happy, in prison, and I daresay they often do; but I feel quite sure they would be still happier in the open air; free to go where they like. Still, people do not always think so; and they like to have a little squirrel in a cage, and try to tame it, and make it amusing and playful. I will tell you a story of a pet squirrel, and then you can make up your mind whether you will choose one of these dear little creatures for your pet or not.

This little fellow was caught in a wood, and brought in a box to a gentleman's house, where a cage was got for it, and everything to make it comfortable and happy was provided. Chestnuts and almonds and acorns were put into the cage for its dinner, and the lady to whom it belonged tried to coax it to come out and feed. But no: it would not move, but sat squeezed up in a corner, and never touched anything that was put before it, or took the smallest notice of anything.

Now, when the lady saw how unhappy it seemed, she was very sorry she had put it into the cage, and wished she could set it free again; but then it was winter-time, and the snow was on the ground, and as the squirrel had been brought from a great distance, she knew that it would not be able to find its way to its old nest, or to make itself a new one.

She therefore determined to

set him free again as soon as the spring came, and till then she would try to make him as happy as she could.

Well, all day long the poor little thing never moved from the corner of the cage; but when the evening came he ventured out, and began to gnaw at the wooden part of his cage.

The lady thought that of course he would never be able to get out in that way, and was, therefore, very much astonished when, with a sudden crash, the side of the cage gave way, and the squirrel bounded into the middle of the room, screaming with joy to find himself really free.

Now, all this happened in the middle of the night, when the lady was in bed; but as she knew that it would be impossible to catch him in the dark, she let him frisk about the room till the morning dawned. And very merry he was, thinking that though it was nothing like so nice as a fir forest, a large room to jump about in was much better than that horrid cage.

His merry pranks, his jumps from one corner of the room to the other, quite prevented his mistress from going to sleep again; so she lay still and watched his gambols; but just as it was growing light, she heard a rattling among the china ornaments on the chimney-piece, and looking up she saw Master Squirrel seated in great state on the top of her favorite vase, looking as happy and contented as if he was once more on the topmost bough of a fir tree.

Every minute she expected

to see it smashed to pieces on the ground; but no: the tiny feet of the squirrel did no harm at all, and with another bound he was soon far away from the treasures on the chimney-piece, only sweeping the dust off them with his long feathery tail as he sprang.

But when morning came, his games were soon over; and though he tried hard to escape, he was once more shut up in his hated cage, never more to be free.

For two days he lay quite still in one corner, never touching his food, nor raising his little head, and the third day he died. Poor little fellow! he could not bear to be a prisoner; and when he found he could not escape, he died of a broken heart.

Now, I do not say that all pet squirrels are as unhappy as this one was; many of them grow quite tame and contented; but I am sure they are always much happier in the woods and fields; indeed, it would be very strange if they were not, for nobody likes to be a prisoner if he can be free. How would you like to be shut up always in a tiny room, and never to stir out of it? Not at all, you say; you like to be able to go where you like, and do what you like. And so does the little squirrel.

And then, when we remember what a short time these little animals have to live, and that they have no new life to begin after death as we have, no long life of happiness in another world; when we remember this, I think we should be very sorry to make their little life here an unhappy one, when it might have been so glad and merry; and I think we should rather try to be as kind to them as we can, remembering that they are God's creatures, and not ours; and that without them our world would not be half so beautiful, or so pleasant and cheerful as it is now.

Now, you know, I told you that the little squirrel when he buries his acorns or chestnuts often forgets where he puts them, and cannot find them again; and that then the little acorn takes root in the ground, and by-and-by there comes up a tree, which grows very tall and very beautiful; and so the little animal that planted it is very useful. And then, after it is dead, we use its fur to make warm muffs, and cloaks to keep us warm in the winter-time. Now, this fur is red in summer-time, and does not look at all like the muffs which we use, but in some cold countries the hair changes color in the winter, and becomes the pretty gray fur which we use so much.

I daresay some of you have got muffs or boas made out of squirrels' fur; if so, did you ever think that that nice soft stuff was once the coat of one of these happy little creatures; the warm coat that God gave it for two reasons — first, that it might be able to bear the cold winds and snowy weather of its native country; and then that when the squirrel had done with it, it might be used to keep you warm? Did you ever think of this? And do you not agree with me that all God's ways are very wonderful? Even in such little things as the squirrel's coat, see how beautifully he has planned it all!

OLD PUSS AND HER LITTLE ONES.

DEAR OLD PUSS.

AND now for a few words about cats. They are so much bigger than any of the other animals that we have been talking about, that I have kept them to the last, because, as our first chapter was about the smallest of little four-legged animals, the mouse, I thought the largest of our little friends should wait till the end.

Now, I am not going to tell you what a cat is like, as I did with the other creatures in this little book, nor am I going to ask you to tell me, for if I did I am sure you would all speak at once, and there would be such a noise that I should not be able to hear a word; for you have seen cats as long as you can remember, and most likely have had many pet cats of your own.

Yes, cats are very common creatures, but I do not think we like them any the less for that; I like to see them in every house, and I think that home would hardly seem like home to us if dear old puss were not there.

Now, there are many different kinds of cats : there are our own tame cats in England, black and white, tabby and tortoiseshell, all of them very pretty ; and then in countries far away there are wild cats, animals which are very like the tame ones, only that they have such a wild, fierce look about their eyes, and sometimes very rough coats. And then there are Smyrna and Persian cats, which have very long, silky fur ; and Egyptian and Nubian cats, which are more like English ones.

A great many years ago, these Egyptian cats were considered very holy, and worshipped as if they were gods. Only think of making a cat into a god, and praying to it!

But the silly Egyptians knew no better, and had many false gods, and perhaps pussy was as good an idol as a block of wood or stone, as neither could do any good or hear any prayers that might be offered to them.

So every family in Egypt had its holy cat, and if any

accident happened, if the house was on fire, the very first thing the people thought of was their precious cat. Till it was safe no one else was thought of; the little children were not of half so much consequence, nor the grown-up people either.

Much as we like our own pussies, we certainly do not think so much of them as this, do we? Oh no! they are very nice, useful pets, but we do not love them as we do each other — not a quarter as much; for they cannot talk to us nor understand what we say to them, as our mammas and papas, brothers and sisters do.

Still they can understand a great deal, can they not? They know quite well if we are angry or pleased with them, and sometimes they almost seem to understand the words we say.

A little child once had a kitten which was a great pet of his, and the two were never so happy as when they were lying on the hearthrug together, kitty being clasped in its little master's arms, with its head pressed against his face. To everybody else puss was very cross, but to little Johnny it was always gentle and loving; and though other people often got scratches and snarls, it never hurt its little master. One day, when a little brother was at play with Johnny, the cat being in the room, though not joining in the game as it often did, in the midst of their romps, puss, who was quietly dosing in a corner, was startled by a loud scream from its little friend. Thinking of course that he must be very much hurt to make such a noise, and that his little playfellow must have done the mischief, the cat flew in a great rage at Johnny's brother, and would very likely have hurt him a great deal, if Johnny had not taken his part, and somehow or other made pussy understand that he had not done any harm at all.

I have heard of another cat that was just as unsociable, and made friends with only one person in the house, refusing to take any notice of any one else. It was called Lee Boo, and had been found, when quite a little kitten, in a hole in the garden wall. It was a beautiful kitten, with a very shiny black coat; and as soon as it was brought into the house, it took a great fancy to a lady who was dressed in black : perhaps it thought she must be a nice person because she wore the same colored clothes as it did. I do not know about that, but ever after it seemed very fond of her, and went with her to every place that she visited.

Sometimes, when she had been out for a walk, and was returning home, Lee Boo would run half-way down the street to meet her; and when she was ill, he sat for hours outside the bedroom door, trying to get in; and if he succeeded, he would jump on the bed and lick his mistress's hand, and purr as loud as he could, to show his joy at seeing her again.

I daresay you are fond of little kittens, and are very pleased when you hear that Mrs. Puss has got some little children — two, three, four, five, or perhaps even six little children. But you are not half so pleased as puss is herself, for she is a very good mother, and is very fond of her little ones, and very proud indeed of them too, sometimes.

A lady who lived in Edinburgh had a very handsome cat which was very fond of her, and had lived with her for some time. After a while, however, puss was packed up in a basket, and sent as a present to a lady living at Glasgow, who received her very kindly, and took great care of her for two months. Then there were two little kittens born, and as puss was very busy taking care of them, her mistress did not watch her quite so much as she had before, for she thought there could be no fear of her running away now.

But she was mistaken: after a few days, the cat and her kittens both vanished. They hunted everywhere for them; but they were gone, and nothing was heard of them for a fortnight.

At last, one day, her first mistress, in Edinburgh, thought she heard pussy's mew at the street-door of her house; and when they opened the door there she was, with both her kittens, safe and sound. I suppose she wanted to show her pretty little children to her old friend; and so she had taken this long journey of forty-four miles, carrying them all the way.

Of course they could not walk, and she could not carry them both at once; so what do you think she did? Several people saw her on the way; and they said she carried one kitten a little way, and then set it down on the ground to wait while she went back to fetch the other; and so she must have walked a great deal more than forty-four miles altogether. No wonder she looked very tired and thin when she reached her journey's end; and how she found her way, I am sure I cannot tell you.

Was she not very persevering and courageous? And should you not like to have known such a wise, clever cat? But cats are always very bold when their little ones are in danger, and I could tell you many, many stories about cats who fought for their children; yes, and got very much hurt in defending them, too.

One bright summer day an

old cat had taken all her family of kittens out for a walk, near the stable which was their home, thinking, I suppose, that the warm sun and nice breeze would do them good.

Now, they were all very happy, never thinking, what a terrible enemy was near; for flying high overhead there was a great hawk, a cruel bird, that lives on tiny birds and animals, and is always on the lookout to catch a chicken or a kitten for his dinner.

Now, though neither the mother nor her children had

seen him, he had seen them, and was watching his opportunity to pounce upon one of them. At last down he came, and had seized one of the kittens, and was flying off with it as fast as possible, when the brave old mother sprang at the cruel hawk, and began a fierce battle for her little one.

The great bird soon found that he could not defend himself and keep his prize too, so dropping the poor bleeding kitten, he turned with all his might on the poor mother. The battle was a terrible one; but puss came off victorious, leaving her enemy dead on the ground. Directly she saw that he was dead, she forgot all about her own wounds, and ran to comfort her poor frightened kitten, licking its sides, and purring as if to soothe its fears, and kissing it to make it well.

How those kittens ought to have loved their mother, and how good they ought to have been! But kittens, like little children, are sometimes very ungrateful to those who take care of them, and forget all the care and love their mothers have shown them ever since they were born; and very likely these little creatures soon forgot their mamma's dreadful battle with the cruel hawk, and the many wounds she got in defending them.

If so, you must not imitate them, but always try and remember all the kindness your mamma has shown to you, and repay her in the only way you can, by loving her, and doing what she tells you.

Sometimes I think that cats and little children are very much alike; they both like very much to be petted, and they both like very much to have their own way; and there is another thing in which pussy is like a little child. If there is a great storm of thunder and lightning, cats often seem very much frightened, and do not like to be alone; and I think too that there are very few children who would not rather have somebody with them when the peals of thunder and the bright flashes of lightning are making them feel rather afraid.

In a family, living in the country, there were once two

very great friends, a cat and a dog; they eat out of the same plate, and often sat close together on the same rug.

After a little while Mrs. Puss had a family of little kittens to take care of, and then she and her charge were lodged in a garret at the top of the house. Of course she stayed most part of the day with her little children, and Pincher, as her friend the dog was called, went up every day to see them, and to inquire how they were.

Well, one day there was a terrible storm of thunder and

lightning, and both Pincher and his friend were very much frightened. The dog came and stayed close to his mistress's side in the drawing-room; but puss very much would have liked to be there too, though she could not leave her little ones all alone in the garret; for only think how terrified they would have been at the sound of the thunder, if their mamma had not been there to comfort them.

But after a little while puss came down stairs and went up to Pincher, looking up in his face and mewing most piteously. The dog took no notice, so she stroked his paw, walked to the door, and stood there mewing, as much as to say, "Do please come with me." Still he would not move; and after trying to make him do as she wished for some time, she gave up in despair, and went up stairs again. After a little while her mistress, hearing her mewing most dismally, went to see what was the matter, and then she found that the poor old mother had been so frightened at the flashes of lightning which came in at the garret window, that she had carried one of her kittens down into a bedroom, and put it into a cupboard: and now she wanted Pincher to take care of that one while she went to fetch the other.

Her mistress did not like to leave the poor thing, as she seemed so frightened, so she stayed with her and her little ones till the storm was over and all was quite quiet again; and they quite forgot all about their terror while she was with them, and were as happy as they could be. The next morning, however, the old cat seemed to have remembered that she had not thanked the lady for her kindness in staying with them the night before; so she got up early, and told her little ones that they must do without her for a little while, because she must go down stairs to do some business. I suppose the dear little kittens promised they would be very good, and not get into any mischief, or fight and quarrel as they did sometimes, for when the lady came out of her room to go down to breakfast, she found Mrs. Puss waiting for her, ready to say Good-morning.

But she had something more to say than that; she had come down on purpose to thank her mistress for her kindness the night before, and so in a very low and gentle voice she mewed out how much obliged she was, and how grateful she felt. But then she was afraid that though the lady was very clever, and knew a great many things much better than she did, yet she might never have learned cat language, and therefore, perhaps, did not understand what she meant by all her gentle, loving mews; so she tried to show by rubbing herself against her, and by purring with all her might, that she had not forgotten how kind she had been to her the night before. And then she followed her down stairs to breakfast, and stayed there till she thought her mistress quite understood what she meant; and then she went back to her kittens quite satisfied.

It is very pleasant to think that even cats know when we

try to make them happy, and that they are grateful for our kindness, and try to show that they are so by their loving ways.

One more story about a cat, and then I must stop, for you must be quite tired, I am sure. This pussy lived in a convent in France, a place where nuns live, and where everything is very quiet and still. No one played with her, nobody took any notice of her, and sometimes, I think, she must have found it very dull.

Now it happened that at dinner-time in the convent a great bell was always rung, and all the nuns went into a large hall and dined together; and when pussy heard it go ding, dong, she ran off too, as fast as her legs would carry her, to the same great hall, where she found her food put ready for her in one corner.

I think she must have been very pleased when she heard the dinner-bell, for it gave her something to do; and, poor thing, she must have often wanted something to do, and some change, for I do not think that even cats like to live all their lives in the same place, with no one to talk to them, and no one to notice them.

Well, one day it happened that when the bell for which pussy listened so eagerly was rung, she was shut up in a room at the top of the house, and could not get out to go down to her dinner. She scratched the door, and whined and mewed most piteously; but it was no use, and for some hours no one thought of her, or found out that she had not had her dinner. At last, to her great joy, the door opened, and she was free. Down stairs she ran, straight to the corner where her dinner was usually placed; but no plate with its nice heap of scraps of meat was to be seen. Poor pussy! how hungry she felt! What was she to do? Must she really wait till the next day before she had anything to eat? Would nobody take pity on her?

No; no one seemed to be thinking about her; everybody else had had dinner, and little thought how hungry and faint the poor cat felt; but we often say that where there's a will there's a way, and as pussy certainly had the will, in a little while she found out the way to get what she wanted.

All at once, on that quiet afternoon, in the old French convent the nuns heard the great dinner-bell begin to ring: slowly and gently it went, as if a very weak hand was pulling the rope; but still it rang on. What could it be ringing for at that time of the day? Something must be the matter, and so they all ran to see what it was. And what did they find, do you think? Why, they found Mrs. Puss hanging to the bell-rope, and pulling away, as if ringing the bell would make her dinner come.

And so it did, for the nuns saw at once what it was she wanted, and pussy got a good meal for her pains. You see she had always heard the bell ring at dinner-time, and so thought, of course, that it had something to do with her getting her food; and as she had been out of the way when it rang before, she thought she would try what pulling it again would do.

I said I would only tell you one more story; but talking of pussy ringing the bell puts me in mind of another, which, as it is very short and funny, I will tell you. This cat did not live in a convent; her home was in the kitchen of a gentleman's house, and her great friend was the cook. Now, Mrs. Cook was very fond of pussy, and very kind to her; but sometimes pussy seemed to think she would rather be alone in the kitchen; for, if the truth must be told, she was a sad thief, and liked to be left by herself, that she might help herself to the good things in the kitchen and pantry.

Now, she had found out that when a certain bell rang the cook went out of the room for a little while, and then she could have a nice feast. But this bell did not ring quite so often as pussy wished; and she began to think whether she could not make it ring sometimes herself. So one day the cook found that the bell called her to the door very often when there was nobody there; and she thought it very strange, and wondered very much what was the reason it rang so often. Just while she was wondering she heard it again, and thought she would look at it before she went to the door. She did so, and what was her surprise when she found Mrs. Puss underneath the bell, every now and then giving a spring and shaking the wire so as to set it going to her heart's content.

But now it is time for you to say good-by to our little animals, and for me to say good-by to my little readers; but before I do so I want to remind you of the text with which we began this little book. You remember what it was, I daresay; you remember that it tells us that no little bird is forgotten by our heavenly Father, however small it may be; and I hope you have not forgotten, too, how often we have noticed God's great love and care for the tiny animals we have been talking about. Well, and if he cares so much, and thinks so much about these little animals whose lives are so short, do you not think he must care a great deal more about little children who have souls that will live forever, either in heaven or hell? Yes, the Bible tells us we are of more value than many sparrows; and as God has given to the little animals and birds their daily food just when they want it, so he has given to us not only all we have need of for our bodies, but Jesus Christ to save our souls. You know this, do you not? Then are you not very thankful to God for all his goodness to you? and, if so, how do you try to show that you are thankful?

The little animals do not know who it is that sends them all their food, and all they want; and yet they are always active and industrious, doing what God has given them to do. Are you as busy as they? Are you trying, like the little squirrel, to gather together a nice little store for the time to come, a store of knowledge for this world and for the world to come? That is the part of the work that God has given you to do: will you not try and do it?

SHELDON & COMPANY'S
JUVENILE BOOKS.

The Harlie Stories. By JACOB ABBOTT. With Illustrations, from Designs by JOHN GILBERT.

6 vols. Price, per vol., 50 cents.

Printed in very large type, for young children.

"These stories are all told in Mr. Abbott's best style, and are most admirable productions."—*Sunday School Times.*

The Rollo Books. By JACOB ABBOTT.

    Rollo Learning to Walk.   Rollo's Museum.
    Rollo Learning to Read.   Rollo's Travels.
    Rollo at Work.   Rollo's Correspondence.
    Rollo at Play.   &c., &c.

14 vols. Illustrated. Uniform style 16mo. Cloth. Price, $12 00.

14 vols. Uniform style. 18mo. Cheap edition. Cloth. Price, $3 75.

Among the multitude of books that have been written for children, none have been more extensively read, and solid enjoyment derived from them, than this series of books. We can remember with what delight we read them in our childhood. To the children of to-day we would say, Be sure and read them; they will both interest and instruct you.

The Oakland Stories. By George B. Taylor. With Illustrations from Designs by H. W. Herrick and others. 16mo. Cloth. Price, $3.60.

Kenny.	Claiborne.
Cousin Guy.	Gustave.

"While in general this story resembles Mr. Abbott's, it is superior to some of that author's later works. It is marked by his best characteristics—the easy, natural dialogue, wholesome, moral, and religious tone, and simple, explanatory style, without being tiresome in repetition. It describes home scenes and suggests home amusements. 'Kenny is seven years old, and for children from seven to twelve, this story is both pleasing and instructive."—*Boston Journal*.

The Cottage Library. By Peter Parley (S. G. Goodrich). 12 vols. 18mo. Price, $7 50.

"There are few persons who have not read with unbounded delight more or less of the books written by Peter Parley, alias S. G. Goodrich. Perhaps no man has ever furnished more instructive and entertaining reading for young people than he."—*Christian Era*.

The Geldart Series. Six choice volumes. By Mrs. Thomas Geldart. With Illustrations from Designs by John Gilbert. 16mo. Price, $3 60.

Daily Thoughts of a Child.	Emilie the Peacemaker.
Truth is Everything.	Sunday Evening Thoughts.
Sunday Morning Thoughts.	Stories of Scotland.

"What children read they often long retain; therefore it is desirable that their books should be of a high moral tone. In this respect Mrs. Geldart has few equals as an author; and we hope that this series will be found in every child's library."—*Worcester Palladium*.

Books Published by Sheldon & Co.

PETER PARLEY'S OWN STORY.

From the Personal Narrative of the late SAMUEL G. GOODRICH (Peter Parley).

1 vol. 16mo, illustrated, price $1.25.

CHILDREN'S SAYINGS;
OR, EARLY LIFE AT HOME.

By CAROLINE HADLEY. With Illustrations, by WALTER CRANE.

1 vol. square 16mo, price 90 cents.

STORIES OF OLD.
OLD TESTAMENT SERIES.

By CAROLINE HADLEY.

1 vol. 12mo, Illustrated, price $1.25.

STORIES OF OLD.
NEW TESTAMENT SERIES.

By CAROLINE HADLEY.

1 vol. 12mo, Illustrated, price $1.25.

ROSE MORTON'S JOURNAL.

A series of volumes containing Rose Morton's Journal for the several months of the year.

Each volume Illustrated, 18mo, 45 cents.

There are now ready,

ROSE MORTON'S JOURNAL FOR JANUARY.
ROSE MORTON'S JOURNAL FOR FEBRUARY.
ROSE MORTON'S JOURNAL FOR MARCH.
ROSE MORTON'S JOURNAL FOR APRIL.
ROSE MORTON'S JOURNAL FOR MAY.

Books Published by Sheldon & Co.

THE ROLLO STORY BOOKS.

By Jacob Abbott.

Trouble on the Mountain,	Georgie,
Causey Building,	Rollo in the Woods,
Apple Gathering,	Rollo's Garden,
The Two Wheelbarrows,	The Steeple Trap,
Blueberrying,	Labor Lost,
The Freshet,	Lucy's Visit.

12 vols. 18mo. Cloth. Illustrated. Price, per set, $4.50

THE FLORENCE STORIES.

By Jacob Abbott.

Vol. 1.—Florence and John. 18mo. Cloth. Illustrated.
Vol. 2.—Grimkie. 18mo. Cloth. Illustrated.
Vol. 3.—The Isle of Wight. 18mo. Cloth. Illustrated.
Vol. 4.—The Orkney Islands. 18mo. Cloth. Illustrated.
Vol. 5.—The English Channel. 18mo. Cloth. Illustrated.
Vol. 6.—Florence's Return. 18mo. Cloth. Illustrated.

Price of each volume $1.00.

From the Boston Journal.

"Mr. Abbott is always an entertaining writer for the young, and this story seems to us to contain more that is really suggestive and instructive than other of his recent productions. Florence and John are children who pursue their studies at home, under the care of their mother, and in the progress of the tale many useful hints are given in regard to home instruction. The main educational idea which runs through all Mr. Abbott's works, that of developing the capacities of children so as to make them self-reliant, is conspicuous in this."

From the New York Observer.

"Mr. Abbott is known to be a pure, successful and useful writer for the young and old. He is also the most popular author of juvenile books now living."

From the Boston Traveller.

"No writer of children's books, not even the renowned Peter Parley, has ever been so successful as Abbott."

Books Published by Sheldon & Company

NEW JUVENILE BOOKS,
To be ready early in the coming Fall.

A NEW SERIES BY AUNT FANNY,
Author of "Nightcap," "Mitten," and "Pet Books."

THE POP-GUN STORIES.
In 6 vols. 16mo., beautifully illustrated.

I.—POP-GUNS.
II.—ONE BIG POP-GUN.
III.—ALL SORTS OF POP-GUNS.
IV.—FUNNY POP-GUNS.
V.—GRASSHOPPER POP-GUNS.
VI.—POST-OFFICE POP-GUNS.

Aunt Fanny is one of the most successful writers for children in this country, as is attested by the very wide sale her previous books have had, and we feel sure that the mere announcement of this new series will attract the attention of her host of admirers.

A NEW SERIES BY T. S. ARTHUR,
Author of "Household Library," and "Arthur's Juvenile Library."

HOME STORIES.
3 vols., 16mo., fully illustrated.

LIST OF VOLUMES.
HIDDEN WINGS.
SOWING THE WIND.
SUNSHINE AT HOME.

The name of this Author is a sufficient Guarantee of the excellence of the Series.

Books Published by Sheldon & Co.

THE BRIGHTHOPE SERIES.

By J. T. TROWBRIDGE.

The Old Battle Ground,	Iron Thorpe,
Father Brighthope,	Burr Cliff.
Hearts and Faces.	

5 vols. 18mo, in cloth, gilt back, uniform. Price $1 00

From the Boston Transcript.

"Mr. Trowbridge has never written anything that was not popular, and each new work has added to his fame. He has a wonderful faculty as a portrayer of New England characteristics, and New England scenes."

From the Salem Register.

"Mr. Trowbridge will find many welcomers to the field of authorship as often as he chooses to enter it, and to leave as pleasant a record behind him as the story of 'Father Brighthope.' The 'Old Battle Ground' is worthy of his reputation as one of the very best portrayers of New England character and describers of New England scenes."

THE GELDART SERIES.

By Mrs. THOMAS GELDART.
5 vols. 16mo. Illustrated by JOHN GILBERT.
Price of each 60 cents.

Daily Thoughts for a Child,	Sunday Evening Thoughts,
Truth is Everything,	Emilie the Peacemaker,
Sunday Morning Thoughts,	cotland

From the Boston Register.

"These charming volumes are the much admired Geldart Series of books for the young, which have established a very enviable reputation in England for their wholesome moral tendency. They are beautifully printed 16mo volumes, with gilt backs, and are sold at 50 cents each. There are five volumes in the series, and they will form a very choice addition to a youth's library."

From the Worcester Palladium.

"What children read they often long retain; therefore it is desirable that their books should be of a high moral tone. In this respect Mrs. Geldart has few equals as an author, and we hope that her works will be found in every child's library."

Books Published by Sheldon & Company.

ROLLO'S TOUR IN EUROPE.

BY JACOB ABBOTT,

Author of the "Rollo Books," "Florence Stories," "American Histories," &c., &c.

ORDER OF THE VOLUMES.

ROLLO ON THE ATLANTIC.
ROLLO IN PARIS.
ROLLO IN SWITZERLAND.
ROLLO IN LONDON.
ROLLO ON THE RHINE.
ROLLO IN SCOTLAND.
ROLLO IN GENEVA.
ROLLO IN HOLLAND.
ROLLO IN NAPLES.
ROLLO IN ROME.

Each volume fully illustrated.
Price per vol., 90 cents.

Mr. Abbott is the most successful writer of books for the young in this, or perhaps, any other country. "ROLLO'S TOUR IN EUROPE," is by far the greatest success of any of Mr. Abbott's works.

From the New York Observer.

"Mr. Abbott is known to be a pure, successful and useful writer for the young and old. He is also the most popular Author of juvenile books now living."

Books Published by Sheldon & Company.

ROLLO'S TOUR IN EUROPE.

BY JACOB ABBOTT,

Author of the "Rollo Books," "Florence Stories," "American Histories," &c., &c.

ORDER OF THE VOLUMES.

ROLLO ON THE ATLANTIC.
ROLLO IN PARIS.
ROLLO IN SWITZERLAND.
ROLLO IN LONDON.
ROLLO ON THE RHINE.
ROLLO IN SCOTLAND.
ROLLO IN GENEVA.
ROLLO IN HOLLAND.
ROLLO IN NAPLES.
ROLLO IN ROME.

Each volume fully illustrated.
Price per vol., 90 cents.

Mr. Abbott is the most successful writer of books for the young in this, or perhaps, any other country. "ROLLO'S TOUR IN EUROPE," is by far the greatest success of any of Mr. Abbott's works.

From the New York Observer.

"Mr. Abbott is known to be a pure, successful and useful writer for the young and old. He is also the most popular Author of juvenile books now living."

www.ingramcontent.com/pod-product-compliance
Lightning Source LLC
Chambersburg PA
CBHW021733220426
43662CB00008B/836